D1373252

The Life Cycle of a
Cow
by Lisa Trumbauer

Consulting Editor: Gail Saunders-Smith, Ph.D.

Consultant: Meg Scott Phipps, Commissioner,
North Carolina Department of Agriculture
and Consumer Services

Pebble Books

an imprint of Capstone Press
Mankato, Minnesota

Pebble Books are published by Capstone Press
151 Good Counsel Drive, P.O. Box 669, Mankato, Minnesota 56002
http://www.capstone-press.com

1 2 3 4 5 6 07 06 05 04 03 02

Library of Congress Cataloging-in-Publication Data
Trumbauer, Lisa, 1963–
    The life cycle of a cow / by Lisa Trumbauer.
    p. cm.—(Life cycles)
    Summary: Simple text and photographs present the life cycle of the cow.
    Includes bibliographical references (p. 23) and index.
    ISBN 0-7368-1451-5 (hardcover)
    1. Cows—Life cycles—Juvenile literature. 2. Cattle—Life cycles—Juvenile
literature. [1. Cows.] I. Title. II. Life cycles (Mankato, Minn.)
SF197.5 .T78 2003
599.64′22—dc21   2002001226

Note to Parents and Teachers

The Life Cycles series supports national science standards related to life science. This book describes and illustrates the life cycle of a Holstein cow. The photographs support early readers in understanding the text. The repetition of words and phrases helps early readers learn new words. This book also introduces early readers to subject-specific vocabulary words, which are defined in the Words to Know section. Early readers may need assistance to read some words and to use the Table of Contents, Words to Know, Read More, Internet Sites, and Index/Word List sections of the book.

Table of Contents

Photographs in this book show the life cycle of a Holstein cow.

1 day

4

A cow begins life
as a calf. The calf is
wet when it is born.

The calf tries to stand
a few minutes after
it is born.

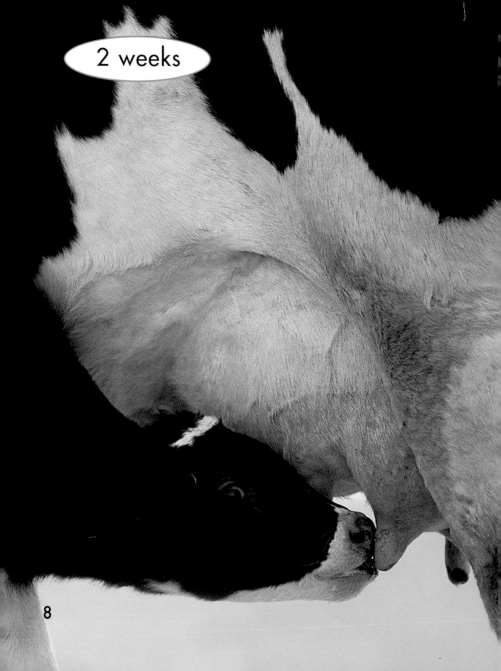

2 weeks

The calf drinks milk
from its mother's body
for two weeks.

2 months

Then the calf eats
hay or grass.

10 months

The calf grows quickly. It becomes strong. It weighs about 600 pounds (270 kilograms).

15 months

The calf becomes an adult after 15 months. Cows can live up to 12 years.

cow

16

bull

Females are called cows.
Males are called bulls.
A cow mates with a bull.

18

A calf grows inside
the cow's body
for nine months.

2 months

1 day

10 months

adult

20

The calf is the start
of a new life cycle.

(Words to Know

bull—an adult male of the cattle family

calf—a young cow; a newborn calf weighs about 90 pounds (40 kilograms).

cow—an adult female of the cattle family

life cycle—the stages of life of an animal; the life cycle includes being born, growing up, having young, and dying.

mate—to join together to produce young

milk—a white liquid made by the bodies of female mammals; female mammals feed milk to their young; a cow feeds milk to a calf for two weeks; she continues to produce milk that humans may drink.

Read More

Bell, Rachael. *Cows.* Farm Animals. Chicago: Heinemann, 2000.

Butterfield, Moira. *Cow.* Who Am I? Mankato, Minn.: Thameside Press, 2000.

Miller, Sara Swan. *Cows.* A True Book. New York: Children's Press, 2000.

Schuh, Mari C. *Cows on the Farm.* On the Farm. Mankato, Minn.: Pebble Books, 2002.

Internet Sites

Barnyard Palace: Dairy Cows
http://www.ncagr.com/cyber/kidswrld/
general/barnyard/dairybn.htm

Kids and Adult Projects
http://www.strausmilk.com/pages/kids.html

Kids Farm: Cattle
http://www.kidsfarm.com/cows.htm

Index/Word List

Word Count: 108
Early-Intervention Level: 12

Editorial Credits

Martha E. H. Rustad, editor; Kia Adams, cover designer; Jennifer Schonborn, interior
designer; Wanda Winch, photo researcher; Karen Risch, product planning editor

Photo Credits

Bruce Coleman Inc./W. Ferchland, 6; Hans Reinhard, 12, 20 (right); Lynn M. Stone,
14, 18; Bradley Simmons, 16 (bottom)
McDonald Wildlife Photography/Joe McDonald, cover (right), 4, 20 (left)
Norvia Behling, 1
PhotoDisc, Inc., cover (left)
Photo Network/Robert Hitchman, 16 (top), 20 (bottom)
Richard Hamilton Smith, 8, 10, 20 (top)